# 50 Premium Seafood Restaurant Recipes for Home

By: Kelly Johnson

# Table of Contents

- Lobster Bisque
- Tuna Tartare
- Oysters Rockefeller
- Shrimp Scampi
- Clam Chowder
- Crab Cakes
- Grilled Swordfish with Lemon Capers
- Blackened Red Snapper
- Seafood Paella
- Mussels in White Wine Sauce
- Pan-Seared Sea Bass with Tomato Basil Relish
- Lobster Newberg
- Thai Green Curry with Shrimp
- Baked Stuffed Clams
- Seared Scallops with Cauliflower Purée
- Spaghetti Vongole (with Clams)
- Sashimi Platter
- Smoked Salmon Gravlax
- Shrimp and Grits
- Crab-Stuffed Portobello Mushrooms
- Miso-Glazed Cod
- Seafood Risotto
- Prawn and Mango Salad
- Mediterranean Octopus Salad
- Lobster Roll
- Grilled Tuna Steaks with Soy Ginger Glaze
- Creamy Crab Pasta
- Ceviche with Lime and Cilantro
- Baked Salmon with Dill and Lemon
- Bouillabaisse (Provençal Fish Stew)
- Fried Calamari with Marinara Sauce
- Garlic Butter Shrimp

- Poke Bowl with Ahi Tuna
- Fish Tacos with Cilantro Lime Slaw
- Lobster Macaroni and Cheese
- Poached Salmon with Dill Sauce
- Crab and Corn Chowder
- Oysters on the Half Shell
- Grilled Sardines with Lemon and Herbs
- Clams Casino
- Curry Crab Legs
- Sautéed Mussels with Garlic and Herbs
- Crab-Stuffed Avocados
- Tuna Poke Nachos
- Spicy Shrimp Tostadas
- Fish en Papillote (Fish in Paper)
- Lobster Ravioli with Sage Butter
- Szechuan Peppercorn Shrimp
- Teriyaki Glazed Salmon
- Seafood Gumbo

**Lobster Bisque**

**Ingredients:**

- 2 lobster tails
- 2 tbsp butter
- 1 onion, finely chopped
- 2 celery stalks, chopped
- 2 garlic cloves, minced
- 1/4 cup tomato paste
- 1/2 cup dry white wine
- 4 cups seafood stock
- 1 cup heavy cream
- 1 tsp paprika
- 1/4 tsp cayenne pepper (optional)
- Salt and pepper to taste
- 2 tbsp flour (optional, for thickening)
- Fresh parsley for garnish

**Instructions:**

1. Cook lobster tails in boiling water for 5-7 minutes, then remove and let cool. Remove the meat and chop into pieces. Set aside.
2. In a pot, melt butter over medium heat. Sauté onion, celery, and garlic until softened.
3. Stir in tomato paste and cook for 2 minutes. Add white wine and cook for another 2 minutes.
4. Add seafood stock and bring to a simmer. Cook for 15 minutes.
5. Blend the mixture until smooth using an immersion blender or by transferring in batches to a blender. Return to the pot.
6. Stir in heavy cream, paprika, cayenne (if using), salt, and pepper. Simmer for 5 minutes.
7. Add lobster meat and cook for another 3 minutes.
8. For extra thickness, you can mix flour with a bit of water and stir it into the bisque, cooking for a few more minutes.
9. Garnish with fresh parsley before serving.

Enjoy your bisque!

# Tuna Tartare

**Ingredients:**

- **For the Tartare:**
    - 8 oz sushi-grade tuna, finely diced
    - 1 avocado, diced
    - 2 tbsp soy sauce
    - 1 tbsp sesame oil
    - 1 tbsp lime juice
    - 1 tsp freshly grated ginger
    - 1 small shallot, finely chopped
    - 1 tbsp chopped fresh cilantro
    - Salt and pepper, to taste
- **For Garnish:**
    - 1 tbsp toasted sesame seeds
    - 1 tbsp finely chopped chives or green onions
    - Sriracha or your favorite hot sauce (optional)
    - Soy sauce, for drizzling (optional)
    - Wonton chips or sliced baguette, for serving

**Instructions:**

1. **Prepare the Tuna:**
    - Dice the sushi-grade tuna into small, uniform cubes. Place it in a mixing bowl.
2. **Mix Ingredients:**
    - Add the avocado cubes to the bowl with the tuna.
    - In a separate small bowl, whisk together the soy sauce, sesame oil, lime juice, ginger, and chopped shallot.
3. **Combine and Season:**
    - Pour the soy sauce mixture over the tuna and avocado. Gently toss to combine.
    - Fold in the chopped cilantro.
    - Season with salt and pepper to taste.
4. **Chill:**
    - Cover and refrigerate the tartare for about 15-20 minutes to let the flavors meld.
5. **Serve:**
    - To plate, you can use a ring mold for a neat presentation or simply spoon the tartare onto plates.
    - Garnish with toasted sesame seeds, chopped chives or green onions, and a drizzle of soy sauce or a dash of sriracha if desired.
6. **Accompaniments:**
    - Serve with crispy wonton chips or slices of toasted baguette for added crunch.

Enjoy your fresh and flavorful tuna tartare!

**Oysters Rockefeller**

**Ingredients:**

- **For the Oysters:**
    - 12 large fresh oysters, shucked and on the half shell
    - Rock salt or coarse sea salt (for serving)
- **For the Rockefeller Topping:**
    - 2 tbsp unsalted butter
    - 1 small shallot, finely chopped
    - 2 cloves garlic, minced
    - 1/2 cup finely chopped spinach (or use a mix of spinach and parsley)
    - 1/4 cup finely chopped celery
    - 1/4 cup breadcrumbs (preferably panko)
    - 1/4 cup grated Parmesan cheese
    - 1/4 cup heavy cream
    - 1/4 tsp ground nutmeg
    - 1/4 tsp cayenne pepper (optional, for heat)
    - Salt and pepper to taste
    - Lemon wedges, for serving

**Instructions:**

1. **Preheat Oven:**
    - Preheat your oven to 425°F (220°C).
2. **Prepare the Oysters:**
    - Arrange the shucked oysters on a baking sheet or in a baking dish on a bed of rock salt to keep them steady.
3. **Make the Rockefeller Topping:**
    - In a skillet, melt the butter over medium heat. Add the shallot and garlic, and sauté until softened, about 2 minutes.
    - Add the chopped spinach and celery. Cook for an additional 2-3 minutes until the spinach is wilted and the mixture is dry.
    - Stir in the breadcrumbs, Parmesan cheese, and heavy cream. Mix well and cook for 1-2 minutes until the mixture is slightly thickened.
    - Season with nutmeg, cayenne pepper (if using), salt, and pepper. Adjust seasoning to taste.
4. **Assemble the Oysters:**
    - Spoon a generous amount of the Rockefeller topping over each oyster.
5. **Bake:**
    - Bake in the preheated oven for 10-12 minutes, or until the topping is golden brown and the oysters are cooked through.
6. **Serve:**
    - Serve immediately with lemon wedges on the side.

Enjoy your rich and flavorful Oysters Rockefeller!

## Shrimp Scampi

### Ingredients:

- 1 lb large shrimp, peeled and deveined
- 8 oz linguine or spaghetti
- 4 tbsp unsalted butter
- 2 tbsp olive oil
- 4 cloves garlic, minced
- 1/4 cup dry white wine (or chicken broth)
- Juice of 1 lemon
- 1/4 tsp red pepper flakes (optional)
- 1/4 cup chopped fresh parsley
- Salt and pepper to taste
- Lemon wedges, for serving

### Instructions:

1. **Cook the Pasta:**
    - Cook the linguine or spaghetti according to package instructions until al dente. Drain and set aside.
2. **Prepare the Shrimp:**
    - In a large skillet, heat the olive oil and 2 tablespoons of butter over medium heat.
    - Add the garlic and cook until fragrant, about 1 minute.
    - Add the shrimp and cook until pink and opaque, about 2-3 minutes per side. Remove shrimp and set aside.
3. **Make the Sauce:**
    - In the same skillet, add the white wine and bring to a simmer, scraping up any bits from the bottom of the pan.
    - Stir in the lemon juice and remaining 2 tablespoons of butter. Cook until the sauce slightly reduces, about 2-3 minutes.
4. **Combine:**
    - Return the shrimp to the skillet and toss to coat in the sauce.
    - Add the cooked pasta to the skillet and toss to combine. Season with red pepper flakes, salt, and pepper to taste.
5. **Serve:**
    - Garnish with chopped parsley and serve with lemon wedges.

Enjoy your delicious shrimp scampi!

## Clam Chowder

### Ingredients:

- 4 oz salt pork or bacon, diced
- 1 medium onion, chopped
- 2 celery stalks, chopped
- 2 cloves garlic, minced
- 3 medium potatoes, peeled and diced
- 2 cups clam juice
- 1 cup chicken broth
- 1 bay leaf
- 1 tsp dried thyme
- 2 cups chopped fresh clams (or canned clams, drained, and juice reserved)
- 1 cup heavy cream
- 2 tbsp all-purpose flour (optional, for thickening)
- Salt and pepper to taste
- Fresh parsley for garnish (optional)

### Instructions:

1. **Cook the Pork:**
   - In a large pot, cook the salt pork or bacon over medium heat until crispy. Remove and set aside, leaving some fat in the pot.
2. **Sauté Vegetables:**
   - Add onion, celery, and garlic to the pot. Cook until softened, about 5 minutes.
3. **Add Potatoes and Liquids:**
   - Stir in the diced potatoes. Add clam juice, chicken broth, bay leaf, and thyme. Bring to a boil, then reduce heat and simmer until potatoes are tender, about 15 minutes.
4. **Add Clams and Cream:**
   - If using flour, mix it with a bit of water to make a slurry, and stir it into the soup to thicken. Add chopped clams and heavy cream. Simmer for 5 minutes until clams are cooked through.
5. **Season and Serve:**
   - Remove bay leaf. Season with salt and pepper to taste. Garnish with crispy salt pork or bacon and fresh parsley if desired.

Serve with oyster crackers or crusty bread. Enjoy your chowder!

## Crab Cakes

### Ingredients:

- 1 lb fresh crab meat (lump or claw)
- 1/2 cup mayonnaise
- 1 egg
- 1 tbsp Dijon mustard
- 1 tbsp Worcestershire sauce
- 1 tsp Old Bay seasoning
- 1/4 cup finely chopped fresh parsley
- 1/4 cup finely chopped onion
- 1/4 cup finely chopped red bell pepper
- 1 cup fresh breadcrumbs
- Salt and pepper to taste
- 2-3 tbsp vegetable oil (for frying)

### Instructions:

1. **Prepare Mixture:**
   - In a large bowl, combine mayonnaise, egg, Dijon mustard, Worcestershire sauce, Old Bay seasoning, parsley, onion, and red bell pepper.
2. **Add Crab Meat:**
   - Gently fold in the crab meat, being careful not to break up the lumps too much. Stir in breadcrumbs until just combined. Season with salt and pepper.
3. **Form Cakes:**
   - Shape the mixture into 8-10 cakes, about 1/2 inch thick.
4. **Cook:**
   - Heat vegetable oil in a skillet over medium heat. Cook crab cakes for 3-4 minutes per side, until golden brown and crispy.
5. **Drain and Serve:**
   - Transfer to paper towels to drain. Serve with a side of tartar sauce or lemon wedges.

Enjoy your crab cakes!

# Grilled Swordfish with Lemon Capers

## Ingredients:

- 4 swordfish steaks (about 6 oz each)
- 2 tbsp olive oil
- 1 lemon, zested and juiced
- 2 cloves garlic, minced
- 2 tbsp capers, drained
- 1/4 cup white wine (optional, can substitute with chicken broth)
- 2 tbsp unsalted butter
- 1 tbsp chopped fresh parsley
- Salt and pepper to taste
- Lemon wedges, for serving

## Instructions:

1. **Marinate Swordfish:**
    - In a small bowl, combine 1 tablespoon olive oil, lemon zest, lemon juice, minced garlic, salt, and pepper.
    - Rub the marinade over the swordfish steaks and let them marinate for about 15-20 minutes.
2. **Preheat Grill:**
    - Preheat your grill to medium-high heat.
3. **Grill Swordfish:**
    - Brush the grill grates with oil to prevent sticking.
    - Grill the swordfish steaks for about 4-5 minutes per side, or until they are cooked through and have nice grill marks. The fish should be opaque and flake easily with a fork.
4. **Make Lemon Caper Sauce:**
    - While the fish is grilling, heat the remaining 1 tablespoon of olive oil in a small saucepan over medium heat.
    - Add the capers and cook for 1-2 minutes.
    - Add the white wine (or chicken broth) and let it simmer for 2-3 minutes until slightly reduced.
    - Stir in the butter until melted and the sauce is slightly thickened.
    - Remove from heat and stir in the chopped parsley.
5. **Serve:**
    - Place the grilled swordfish on plates and spoon the lemon caper sauce over the top.
    - Serve with lemon wedges on the side.

Enjoy your delicious grilled swordfish with a zesty lemon caper sauce!

**Blackened Red Snapper**

**Ingredients:**

- 4 red snapper fillets (about 6 oz each)
- 2 tbsp olive oil (or melted butter)
- 1 tbsp paprika
- 1 tsp cayenne pepper
- 1 tsp onion powder
- 1 tsp garlic powder
- 1 tsp dried thyme
- 1 tsp dried oregano
- 1/2 tsp ground black pepper
- 1/2 tsp salt
- 1/4 tsp white pepper (optional)
- Lemon wedges, for serving

**Instructions:**

1. **Prepare the Spice Mix:**
    - In a small bowl, combine paprika, cayenne pepper, onion powder, garlic powder, dried thyme, dried oregano, black pepper, salt, and white pepper.
2. **Season the Fish:**
    - Pat the red snapper fillets dry with paper towels.
    - Rub the fillets with olive oil or melted butter on both sides.
    - Generously coat the fillets with the spice mix, pressing it in slightly to adhere.
3. **Preheat Skillet:**
    - Heat a cast-iron skillet or heavy-bottomed pan over high heat until very hot. This helps to create a nice sear and blackened crust.
4. **Cook the Fish:**
    - Add a small amount of oil to the hot skillet, then carefully place the fillets in the pan. Avoid overcrowding the pan—cook in batches if necessary.
    - Cook the fillets for about 3-4 minutes per side, or until the exterior is blackened and crispy, and the fish flakes easily with a fork.
5. **Serve:**
    - Transfer the fillets to a plate and let them rest for a few minutes.
    - Serve with lemon wedges on the side.

Enjoy your blackened red snapper with a side of your choice, such as a fresh salad, rice, or roasted vegetables!

**Seafood Paella**

**Ingredients:**

- 1/4 cup olive oil
- 1 onion, finely chopped
- 1 bell pepper, chopped
- 4 cloves garlic, minced
- 1 1/2 cups paella or short-grain rice
- 1/2 tsp saffron threads (or 1 tsp saffron powder)
- 1 tsp smoked paprika
- 1/2 tsp dried thyme
- 1/2 tsp dried oregano
- 1 cup diced tomatoes (fresh or canned)
- 3 cups seafood stock or chicken broth
- 1 cup white wine (optional)
- 12 large shrimp, peeled and deveined
- 12 mussels, cleaned and debearded
- 12 clams, cleaned
- 1 cup frozen peas
- 1 lemon, cut into wedges
- Fresh parsley, chopped (for garnish)

**Instructions:**

1. **Prepare the Base:**
   - Heat olive oil in a large paella pan or wide skillet over medium heat.
   - Sauté onion and bell pepper until softened, about 5 minutes.
   - Add garlic and cook for 1 minute until fragrant.
2. **Add Rice and Spices:**
   - Stir in the rice, saffron, smoked paprika, thyme, and oregano, coating the rice with the oil and spices.
   - Cook for 1-2 minutes, stirring occasionally.
3. **Add Liquids and Tomatoes:**
   - Add the diced tomatoes, seafood stock (or chicken broth), and white wine (if using). Bring to a simmer.
   - Reduce heat to medium-low and cook uncovered for about 15 minutes, or until the rice is almost tender and the liquid is mostly absorbed.
4. **Add Seafood:**
   - Arrange shrimp, mussels, and clams on top of the rice.
   - Cover the pan with a lid or foil and cook for an additional 10 minutes, or until the seafood is cooked through and the shells have opened. Discard any unopened shells.
5. **Finish and Serve:**

- Stir in the frozen peas and cook for another 2 minutes.
- Garnish with fresh parsley and serve with lemon wedges.

Enjoy your delicious seafood paella!

**Mussels in White Wine Sauce**

**Ingredients:**

- 2 lbs fresh mussels, cleaned and debearded
- 2 tbsp olive oil
- 4 cloves garlic, minced
- 1 shallot, finely chopped
- 1 cup white wine (dry white wine or Chardonnay)
- 1 cup chicken broth
- 1/4 cup chopped fresh parsley
- 1/4 cup heavy cream (optional, for a richer sauce)
- 1 lemon, juiced
- Salt and pepper to taste
- Crusty bread, for serving

**Instructions:**

1. **Prepare the Mussels:**
   - Rinse mussels under cold water, scrubbing the shells and removing any beards. Discard any mussels that are cracked or do not close when tapped.
2. **Cook Aromatics:**
   - Heat olive oil in a large pot or Dutch oven over medium heat.
   - Add garlic and shallot, sautéing until softened, about 2 minutes.
3. **Add Liquids:**
   - Pour in the white wine and chicken broth. Bring to a simmer and cook for 2-3 minutes to allow the alcohol to evaporate slightly.
4. **Cook Mussels:**
   - Add the mussels to the pot, cover, and cook for 5-7 minutes, or until the mussels have opened. Discard any that remain closed.
5. **Finish the Sauce:**
   - Stir in the chopped parsley and heavy cream, if using. Cook for another 1-2 minutes.
   - Season with lemon juice, salt, and pepper to taste.
6. **Serve:**
   - Serve the mussels with the sauce over crusty bread or with a side of your choice.

Enjoy your mussels in a flavorful white wine sauce!

## Pan-Seared Sea Bass with Tomato Basil Relish

**Ingredients:**

- **For the Sea Bass:**
    - 4 sea bass fillets (about 6 oz each), skin on
    - 2 tbsp olive oil
    - Salt and pepper to taste
- **For the Tomato Basil Relish:**
    - 2 cups cherry or grape tomatoes, halved
    - 1/4 cup red onion, finely chopped
    - 2 tbsp fresh basil, chopped
    - 1 tbsp extra virgin olive oil
    - 1 tbsp balsamic vinegar
    - 1 clove garlic, minced
    - Salt and pepper to taste

**Instructions:**

1. **Prepare the Relish:**
    - In a medium bowl, combine cherry tomatoes, red onion, basil, olive oil, balsamic vinegar, and minced garlic.
    - Season with salt and pepper. Mix well and set aside to let the flavors meld.
2. **Prepare the Sea Bass:**
    - Pat the sea bass fillets dry with paper towels. Season both sides with salt and pepper.
    - Heat olive oil in a large skillet over medium-high heat.
3. **Cook the Sea Bass:**
    - Place the fillets skin-side down in the hot skillet. Cook for 4-5 minutes without moving them, until the skin is crispy and the fish is cooked about three-quarters of the way through.
    - Flip the fillets and cook for an additional 2-3 minutes, or until the fish is cooked through and flakes easily with a fork.
4. **Serve:**
    - Place the sea bass fillets on plates and top with the tomato basil relish.
    - Garnish with additional basil if desired.

Enjoy your pan-seared sea bass with the fresh and tangy tomato basil relish!

# Lobster Newberg

**Ingredients:**

- 2 lobsters (about 1.5 lbs each)
- 2 tbsp unsalted butter
- 1/2 cup finely chopped onion
- 1/2 cup finely chopped mushrooms
- 2 cloves garlic, minced
- 1/4 cup dry white wine
- 1 cup heavy cream
- 3 large egg yolks
- 1/4 tsp cayenne pepper (optional)
- 1/4 cup brandy (optional, for a richer flavor)
- 1/2 cup grated Gruyère or Swiss cheese
- Salt and pepper to taste
- 2 tbsp chopped fresh parsley (for garnish)
- Toasted bread or puff pastry shells, for serving

**Instructions:**

1. **Prepare the Lobster:**
    - Boil lobsters in a large pot of salted water for about 8-10 minutes. Let cool, then remove the meat from the shells and cut into bite-sized pieces. Set aside.
2. **Cook Aromatics:**
    - In a large skillet, melt butter over medium heat. Add onions, mushrooms, and garlic. Sauté until softened, about 5 minutes.
3. **Make the Sauce:**
    - Add white wine to the skillet and cook until reduced by half.
    - Stir in the heavy cream and cook until the mixture thickens slightly.
4. **Combine Ingredients:**
    - In a bowl, whisk egg yolks. Gradually stir in a small amount of the hot cream mixture to temper the yolks, then slowly stir the yolk mixture back into the skillet.
    - Add lobster meat, cayenne pepper (if using), and brandy (if using). Cook for another 2-3 minutes, until heated through. Stir in the grated cheese until melted and combined. Season with salt and pepper.
5. **Serve:**
    - Spoon the Lobster Newberg over toasted bread or into puff pastry shells.
    - Garnish with chopped parsley.

Enjoy your luxurious Lobster Newberg!

**Thai Green Curry with Shrimp**

**Ingredients:**

- **For the Curry:**
    - 1 lb large shrimp, peeled and deveined
    - 2 tbsp vegetable oil
    - 3-4 tbsp green curry paste (adjust to taste)
    - 1 can (14 oz) coconut milk
    - 1 cup chicken or vegetable broth
    - 1 tbsp fish sauce
    - 1 tbsp palm sugar or brown sugar
    - 1-2 Thai bird chilies, sliced (optional, for extra heat)
    - 1 red bell pepper, sliced
    - 1 cup snap peas or green beans
    - 1 cup bamboo shoots, sliced (optional)
    - 1/2 cup Thai basil leaves (or fresh basil if unavailable)
    - Juice of 1 lime
    - Salt to taste
- **For Garnish:**
    - Fresh cilantro, chopped
    - Lime wedges

**Instructions:**

1. **Prepare the Shrimp:**
    - In a bowl, season the shrimp with a pinch of salt and set aside.
2. **Cook the Curry Paste:**
    - Heat the vegetable oil in a large pan or wok over medium heat.
    - Add the green curry paste and cook for 1-2 minutes, stirring constantly until fragrant.
3. **Add Liquids and Vegetables:**
    - Pour in the coconut milk and chicken or vegetable broth. Stir well to combine.
    - Add the fish sauce, sugar, and bird chilies (if using). Bring to a simmer.
4. **Add Vegetables:**
    - Add the red bell pepper, snap peas or green beans, and bamboo shoots (if using). Cook for 3-4 minutes, or until the vegetables are tender but still crisp.
5. **Cook the Shrimp:**
    - Add the shrimp to the pan. Cook for 2-3 minutes, or until the shrimp turn pink and are cooked through.
6. **Finish the Curry:**
    - Stir in the Thai basil leaves and lime juice. Adjust seasoning with salt or additional fish sauce if needed.
7. **Serve:**

- Serve the curry over jasmine rice or with rice noodles.
- Garnish with fresh cilantro and lime wedges.

Enjoy your delicious Thai green curry with shrimp!

**Baked Stuffed Clams**

**Ingredients:**

- **For the Stuffing:**
    - 12 large clams (littleneck or cherrystone), cleaned and scrubbed
    - 4 tbsp unsalted butter
    - 1/2 cup finely chopped onion
    - 2 cloves garlic, minced
    - 1/2 cup breadcrumbs (preferably panko)
    - 1/4 cup grated Parmesan cheese
    - 1/4 cup chopped fresh parsley
    - 1/4 cup finely chopped celery
    - 1/4 cup clam juice (reserved from the clams)
    - 1/2 tsp dried thyme
    - 1/2 tsp dried oregano
    - 1/4 tsp red pepper flakes (optional)
    - Salt and pepper to taste
    - Lemon wedges, for serving

**Instructions:**

1. **Preheat Oven:**
    - Preheat your oven to 375°F (190°C).
2. **Prepare the Clams:**
    - In a large pot, steam the clams in a bit of water until they open, about 5-7 minutes. Discard any that do not open.
    - Remove the clams from their shells, finely chop the clam meat, and set aside. Reserve the shells for stuffing.
3. **Make the Stuffing:**
    - In a skillet, melt butter over medium heat. Add onion and celery, cooking until softened, about 5 minutes.
    - Stir in garlic and cook for an additional 1 minute.
    - Remove from heat and add breadcrumbs, Parmesan cheese, parsley, chopped clam meat, clam juice, thyme, oregano, and red pepper flakes (if using). Mix well. Season with salt and pepper.
4. **Stuff the Clams:**
    - Spoon the stuffing mixture into the reserved clam shells, pressing down slightly to pack it in.
5. **Bake:**
    - Arrange the stuffed clams on a baking sheet and bake for 15-20 minutes, or until the tops are golden and crispy.
6. **Serve:**
    - Serve the baked stuffed clams with lemon wedges.

Enjoy your flavorful and crispy baked stuffed clams!

# Seared Scallops with Cauliflower Purée

**Ingredients:**

- **For the Cauliflower Purée:**
    - 1 large head of cauliflower, cut into florets
    - 2 tbsp unsalted butter
    - 1/2 cup heavy cream
    - 1 cup chicken or vegetable broth
    - Salt and pepper to taste
- **For the Seared Scallops:**
    - 12 large sea scallops, patted dry
    - 2 tbsp olive oil
    - Salt and freshly ground black pepper
    - 1 tbsp unsalted butter
    - 1 garlic clove, minced (optional)
    - Lemon wedges, for garnish

**Instructions:**

1. **Prepare the Cauliflower Purée:**
    - Steam or boil the cauliflower florets until tender, about 10 minutes.
    - Drain and transfer to a blender or food processor.
    - Add butter, heavy cream, and chicken or vegetable broth. Blend until smooth and creamy. Adjust seasoning with salt and pepper. If the purée is too thick, you can add a bit more cream or broth to reach the desired consistency. Keep warm.
2. **Prepare the Scallops:**
    - Pat the scallops dry with paper towels to remove excess moisture. This helps achieve a good sear.
    - Season both sides of the scallops with salt and pepper.
3. **Sear the Scallops:**
    - Heat olive oil in a large skillet over medium-high heat.
    - Once the oil is hot, add the scallops to the skillet. Avoid overcrowding—cook in batches if necessary.
    - Sear the scallops for about 2-3 minutes per side, or until a golden-brown crust forms and the scallops are opaque in the center. Be careful not to overcook them.
    - If desired, add a tablespoon of butter and minced garlic to the pan during the last minute of cooking and baste the scallops with the melted butter.
4. **Serve:**
    - Spoon a generous amount of cauliflower purée onto each plate.
    - Arrange the seared scallops on top of the purée.
    - Garnish with a lemon wedge and, if desired, a sprinkle of fresh herbs or microgreens.

Enjoy your elegant seared scallops with creamy cauliflower purée!

## Spaghetti Vongole (with Clams)

### Ingredients:

- 1 lb (450g) spaghetti
- 2 lbs (900g) fresh clams (littleneck or manila), cleaned and scrubbed
- 3 tbsp olive oil
- 4 cloves garlic, thinly sliced
- 1/4 tsp red pepper flakes (optional, for a bit of heat)
- 1 cup dry white wine
- 1/4 cup chopped fresh parsley
- Juice of 1 lemon
- Salt and freshly ground black pepper, to taste
- Lemon wedges, for serving

### Instructions:

1. **Prepare the Clams:**
    - In a large bowl, soak the clams in cold water with a bit of salt for about 30 minutes to help them purge any sand. Rinse under cold water and scrub the shells if needed.
2. **Cook the Spaghetti:**
    - Bring a large pot of salted water to a boil. Cook the spaghetti according to the package instructions until al dente. Reserve 1/2 cup of pasta cooking water, then drain the spaghetti and set aside.
3. **Cook the Clams:**
    - Heat olive oil in a large skillet or sauté pan over medium heat.
    - Add garlic and red pepper flakes (if using) and sauté until garlic is fragrant but not browned, about 1-2 minutes.
    - Add the clams to the skillet and pour in the white wine. Increase the heat to high and cover the pan.
    - Cook until the clams open, about 5-7 minutes. Discard any clams that do not open.
4. **Combine Pasta and Clams:**
    - Remove the clams from the skillet with a slotted spoon and set aside.
    - Add the drained spaghetti to the skillet, tossing to coat in the sauce. If needed, add some of the reserved pasta cooking water to help create a smooth sauce.
    - Stir in the lemon juice and chopped parsley. Season with salt and pepper to taste.
5. **Serve:**
    - Divide the spaghetti among serving plates. Top with the cooked clams.
    - Garnish with additional parsley and serve with lemon wedges on the side.

Enjoy your classic and flavorful Spaghetti Vongole!

# Sashimi Platter

**Ingredients:**

- **Sashimi:**
    - 4 oz fresh tuna (ahi or yellowfin), sliced into thin, even pieces
    - 4 oz fresh salmon, sliced into thin, even pieces
    - 4 oz fresh yellowtail or sea bream, sliced into thin, even pieces
    - 4 oz fresh shrimp (if available), cooked and chilled
    - Optional: 4 oz scallops, sliced thinly
- **Accompaniments:**
    - 1 cup pickled ginger
    - 1/2 cup wasabi
    - 1/2 cup soy sauce or tamari
    - 1-2 sheets of nori, cut into strips
    - 1 cucumber, thinly sliced
    - 1 radish, thinly sliced
    - Lemon or lime wedges, for garnish
- **For Garnish:**
    - Fresh cilantro or shiso leaves
    - Microgreens or edible flowers (optional)

**Instructions:**

1. **Prepare the Seafood:**
    - Ensure all fish is extremely fresh and has been sourced from a reputable supplier. Keep it chilled until ready to serve.
    - Slice the seafood into thin, even pieces. For tuna and salmon, aim for 1/4-inch thick slices. For shrimp, slice in half lengthwise if they are large.
2. **Arrange the Platter:**
    - On a large serving platter or board, arrange the sashimi slices artfully. You can group different types together or arrange them in a pattern.
    - Add the cooked shrimp and scallops (if using) to the platter.
3. **Add Accompaniments:**
    - Place small bowls of pickled ginger, wasabi, and soy sauce around the platter.
    - Arrange the nori strips, cucumber slices, and radish slices around the sashimi for added texture and color.
    - Garnish with lemon or lime wedges, fresh cilantro or shiso leaves, and optional microgreens or edible flowers.
4. **Serve:**
    - Serve immediately with chopsticks or small tongs for easy picking.

Enjoy your elegant and delicious sashimi platter!

## Smoked Salmon Gravlax

### Ingredients:

- 1 lb (450g) fresh salmon fillet, skin-on
- 1/4 cup sea salt
- 1/4 cup sugar
- 1 tbsp freshly ground black pepper
- 1 tbsp crushed coriander seeds
- 1 tbsp chopped fresh dill (or 2 tbsp dried dill)
- 1 lemon, zested
- 1 tbsp vodka or aquavit (optional, for added flavor)

### Instructions:

1. **Prepare the Cure Mix:**
   - In a bowl, combine sea salt, sugar, black pepper, crushed coriander seeds, chopped dill, and lemon zest.
2. **Prepare the Salmon:**
   - Rinse the salmon fillet under cold water and pat dry with paper towels.
   - Place the salmon on a large piece of plastic wrap or parchment paper.
3. **Apply the Cure:**
   - Rub the cure mixture evenly over the surface of the salmon. If using vodka or aquavit, drizzle it over the salmon before applying the cure.
4. **Wrap and Refrigerate:**
   - Wrap the salmon tightly in the plastic wrap or parchment paper. Place the wrapped salmon in a shallow dish to catch any drips.
   - Refrigerate for 2-3 days, turning the salmon once a day.
5. **Slice and Serve:**
   - After curing, remove the salmon from the wrap and gently rinse off the cure mixture. Pat dry with paper towels.
   - Slice the salmon thinly at an angle, using a sharp knife.
6. **Serve:**
   - Serve the gravlax with thinly sliced rye bread, mustard sauce, capers, and additional fresh dill if desired.

Enjoy your homemade smoked salmon gravlax!

**Shrimp and Grits**

**Ingredients:**

- **For the Grits:**
    - 1 cup stone-ground grits
    - 4 cups water or chicken broth
    - 1 cup milk or heavy cream
    - 2 tbsp unsalted butter
    - 1 cup shredded sharp cheddar cheese
    - Salt and pepper to taste
- **For the Shrimp:**
    - 1 lb large shrimp, peeled and deveined
    - 4 tbsp unsalted butter
    - 4 cloves garlic, minced
    - 1/2 cup chicken broth
    - 1/4 cup lemon juice
    - 1/4 cup chopped fresh parsley
    - 1/2 tsp smoked paprika
    - 1/2 tsp cayenne pepper (optional, for heat)
    - Salt and pepper to taste
    - 4 slices bacon, chopped (optional, for added flavor)
    - 1/2 cup diced tomatoes (optional, for extra freshness)

**Instructions:**

1. **Prepare the Grits:**
    - In a medium saucepan, bring water or chicken broth to a boil.
    - Gradually whisk in the grits. Reduce heat to low, cover, and simmer for 20-25 minutes, stirring occasionally, until the grits are tender.
    - Stir in milk or cream, butter, and cheese. Season with salt and pepper. Keep warm.
2. **Cook the Bacon (if using):**
    - In a large skillet, cook the chopped bacon over medium heat until crispy. Remove with a slotted spoon and set aside. Leave the bacon drippings in the pan.
3. **Prepare the Shrimp:**
    - In the same skillet, add butter to the bacon drippings and melt over medium heat.
    - Add minced garlic and cook until fragrant, about 1 minute.
    - Add the shrimp and cook for 2-3 minutes per side, or until they are pink and cooked through.
    - Remove the shrimp from the skillet and set aside.
4. **Make the Sauce:**

- In the same skillet, add chicken broth, lemon juice, smoked paprika, and cayenne pepper (if using). Cook for 2-3 minutes, scraping up any browned bits from the bottom of the pan.
- Return the shrimp to the skillet, along with the chopped bacon and diced tomatoes if using. Toss to coat in the sauce. Stir in chopped parsley. Adjust seasoning with salt and pepper.

5. **Serve:**
    - Spoon the grits onto plates or bowls. Top with the shrimp and sauce.

Enjoy your delicious shrimp and grits!

# Crab-Stuffed Portobello Mushrooms

## Ingredients:

- 4 large Portobello mushrooms, stems removed and cleaned
- 2 tbsp olive oil
- 1/2 cup finely chopped onion
- 2 cloves garlic, minced
- 1/2 cup breadcrumbs (preferably panko)
- 1/2 cup grated Parmesan cheese
- 1/4 cup chopped fresh parsley
- 1 tbsp lemon juice
- 8 oz crabmeat, picked over for shells
- 1/4 cup mayonnaise
- 1/4 cup sour cream or heavy cream
- 1 tsp Dijon mustard
- 1/2 tsp Old Bay seasoning or seafood seasoning
- Salt and freshly ground black pepper to taste
- 1/4 cup shredded mozzarella or Gruyère cheese (optional, for topping)

## Instructions:

1. **Prepare the Mushrooms:**
    - Preheat your oven to 375°F (190°C).
    - Brush the Portobello mushrooms with olive oil on both sides and season with salt and pepper. Place them on a baking sheet, gill side up.
2. **Cook the Aromatics:**
    - In a skillet, heat 1 tbsp olive oil over medium heat.
    - Add the chopped onion and cook until softened, about 4-5 minutes.
    - Add the garlic and cook for an additional 1 minute until fragrant. Remove from heat.
3. **Make the Crab Filling:**
    - In a large bowl, combine breadcrumbs, grated Parmesan cheese, chopped parsley, and lemon juice.
    - Gently fold in the crabmeat.
    - In a small bowl, mix together mayonnaise, sour cream (or heavy cream), Dijon mustard, and Old Bay seasoning. Add this mixture to the crabmeat and mix until well combined. Adjust seasoning with salt and pepper.
4. **Stuff the Mushrooms:**
    - Spoon the crab mixture into each mushroom cap, pressing it down slightly to pack it in.
    - If using, sprinkle shredded mozzarella or Gruyère cheese on top of each stuffed mushroom.
5. **Bake:**

- Bake in the preheated oven for 15-20 minutes, or until the mushrooms are tender and the topping is golden brown.
6. **Serve:**
    - Garnish with additional chopped parsley if desired and serve warm.

Enjoy your delicious and elegant crab-stuffed Portobello mushrooms!

**Miso-Glazed Cod**

**Ingredients:**

- 4 cod fillets (6 oz each), skinless
- 1/4 cup white miso paste
- 2 tbsp sake (or dry white wine)
- 2 tbsp mirin (or honey)
- 2 tbsp soy sauce
- 2 tbsp brown sugar
- 1 tbsp rice vinegar
- 1 tbsp grated ginger
- 2 cloves garlic, minced
- 1 tbsp vegetable oil
- Sesame seeds, for garnish
- Thinly sliced green onions, for garnish

**Instructions:**

1. **Prepare the Marinade:**
    - In a bowl, whisk together miso paste, sake, mirin, soy sauce, brown sugar, rice vinegar, grated ginger, and minced garlic until smooth.
2. **Marinate the Cod:**
    - Place the cod fillets in a resealable plastic bag or shallow dish. Pour the marinade over the fillets, ensuring they are well coated.
    - Refrigerate and marinate for at least 30 minutes, or up to 2 hours for more flavor.
3. **Preheat Oven:**
    - Preheat your oven to 400°F (200°C).
4. **Cook the Cod:**
    - Remove the cod from the marinade and let excess drip off.
    - Heat vegetable oil in an oven-safe skillet over medium-high heat.
    - Sear the cod fillets for about 2-3 minutes on each side, until golden brown.
5. **Finish in the Oven:**
    - Transfer the skillet to the preheated oven and bake for 8-10 minutes, or until the cod flakes easily with a fork.
6. **Garnish and Serve:**
    - Garnish with sesame seeds and sliced green onions. Serve with steamed rice or vegetables.

Enjoy your delicious and flavorful miso-glazed cod!

**Seafood Risotto**

**Ingredients:**

- 1 lb mixed seafood (such as shrimp, scallops, and clams), cleaned and prepared
- 4 cups seafood stock or chicken broth (preferably homemade or low-sodium)
- 1 cup dry white wine
- 1 1/2 cups Arborio rice
- 2 tbsp olive oil
- 1 small onion, finely chopped
- 2 cloves garlic, minced
- 1/2 cup dry white wine
- 1/2 cup grated Parmesan cheese
- 2 tbsp unsalted butter
- 1/4 cup chopped fresh parsley
- Salt and freshly ground black pepper to taste
- Lemon wedges, for garnish

**Instructions:**

1. **Prepare the Seafood:**
   - If using raw shrimp, scallops, and clams, cook them separately before adding them to the risotto. For shrimp and scallops, sear them in a hot pan with a bit of olive oil until cooked through (about 2-3 minutes per side). For clams, steam them in a pot with a bit of water until they open (discard any that do not open). Set all seafood aside.
2. **Prepare the Broth:**
   - In a saucepan, keep the seafood stock or chicken broth warm over low heat.
3. **Cook the Risotto:**
   - In a large, heavy-bottomed skillet or Dutch oven, heat olive oil over medium heat.
   - Add the chopped onion and cook until translucent, about 4-5 minutes.
   - Stir in the minced garlic and cook for another minute until fragrant.
   - Add the Arborio rice and cook for 1-2 minutes, stirring constantly until the rice is lightly toasted.
4. **Deglaze and Simmer:**
   - Pour in the white wine and cook, stirring frequently, until the wine is mostly absorbed.
   - Begin adding the warm broth one ladleful at a time, stirring continuously and allowing each addition to be absorbed before adding the next. Continue this process until the rice is creamy and al dente, about 18-20 minutes.
5. **Add Seafood and Finish:**
   - When the risotto is almost done, stir in the cooked seafood and cook for an additional 2-3 minutes to heat through.

- Remove from heat and stir in the grated Parmesan cheese and butter. Season with salt and pepper to taste.
6. **Serve:**
    - Spoon the risotto onto plates or into bowls.
    - Garnish with chopped parsley and lemon wedges.

Enjoy your creamy and flavorful seafood risotto!

# Prawn and Mango Salad

## Ingredients:

- **For the Salad:**
    - 1 lb (450g) large prawns, peeled and deveined
    - 1 ripe mango, peeled and diced
    - 4 cups mixed salad greens (such as arugula, spinach, and lettuce)
    - 1/2 cucumber, thinly sliced
    - 1 red bell pepper, thinly sliced
    - 1/4 red onion, thinly sliced
    - 1 avocado, diced
    - 1/4 cup fresh cilantro or mint, chopped
- **For the Dressing:**
    - 3 tbsp olive oil
    - 2 tbsp lime juice (or lemon juice)
    - 1 tbsp honey or agave syrup
    - 1 tsp soy sauce or tamari
    - 1 clove garlic, minced
    - Salt and freshly ground black pepper to taste

## Instructions:

1. **Prepare the Prawns:**
    - Heat a grill pan or skillet over medium-high heat.
    - Season the prawns with a bit of salt and pepper.
    - Cook the prawns for 2-3 minutes per side, until they turn pink and opaque. Remove from heat and let cool slightly.
2. **Prepare the Salad Ingredients:**
    - In a large salad bowl, combine the mixed greens, diced mango, cucumber, red bell pepper, red onion, and avocado.
3. **Make the Dressing:**
    - In a small bowl or jar, whisk together olive oil, lime juice, honey, soy sauce, minced garlic, salt, and pepper until well combined.
4. **Assemble the Salad:**
    - Add the cooked prawns to the salad bowl.
    - Drizzle the dressing over the salad and toss gently to combine.
5. **Garnish and Serve:**
    - Sprinkle chopped cilantro or mint over the salad before serving.

Enjoy your vibrant and delicious prawn and mango salad!

# Mediterranean Octopus Salad

**Ingredients:**

- 1 lb (450g) octopus, cleaned
- 1/4 cup olive oil
- 2 tbsp red wine vinegar or lemon juice
- 2 cloves garlic, minced
- 1 tsp dried oregano
- 1/2 tsp smoked paprika
- Salt and freshly ground black pepper to taste
- 1 cup cherry tomatoes, halved
- 1/2 cucumber, sliced
- 1/4 red onion, thinly sliced
- 1/4 cup Kalamata olives, pitted and halved
- 1/4 cup crumbled feta cheese
- Fresh parsley, chopped (for garnish)

**Instructions:**

1. **Cook the Octopus:**
    - Bring a large pot of salted water to a boil. Add the octopus and simmer for about 45-60 minutes, or until tender. You can also use a pressure cooker to reduce cooking time.
    - Once cooked, let the octopus cool slightly, then slice it into bite-sized pieces.
2. **Prepare the Dressing:**
    - In a small bowl, whisk together olive oil, red wine vinegar or lemon juice, minced garlic, dried oregano, smoked paprika, salt, and pepper.
3. **Assemble the Salad:**
    - In a large bowl, combine the sliced octopus, cherry tomatoes, cucumber, red onion, and Kalamata olives.
    - Drizzle the dressing over the salad and toss gently to coat.
4. **Finish and Serve:**
    - Sprinkle crumbled feta cheese and chopped parsley over the top.
    - Serve chilled or at room temperature.

Enjoy your Mediterranean octopus salad!

## Lobster Roll

**Ingredients:**

- **For the Lobster Filling:**
    - 1 1/2 lbs (680g) lobster tails (about 3-4 tails), cooked and shelled
    - 1/4 cup mayonnaise
    - 1 tbsp lemon juice
    - 1 tbsp chopped fresh chives (or parsley)
    - 1 tbsp chopped celery (optional)
    - 1 tsp Dijon mustard
    - Salt and freshly ground black pepper to taste
- **For the Rolls:**
    - 4 hot dog or split-top rolls
    - 2 tbsp unsalted butter
    - Lemon wedges, for serving
    - Extra chives or parsley, for garnish

**Instructions:**

1. **Prepare the Lobster:**
    - Bring a large pot of salted water to a boil. Cook the lobster tails for 6-8 minutes until they turn bright red and the meat is opaque. Remove from the pot and let cool.
    - Once cooled, remove the lobster meat from the shells and cut it into bite-sized pieces.
2. **Make the Lobster Filling:**
    - In a bowl, combine the mayonnaise, lemon juice, chopped chives, celery (if using), and Dijon mustard.
    - Gently fold in the lobster meat. Season with salt and pepper to taste.
3. **Prepare the Rolls:**
    - Heat a skillet over medium heat. Spread the inside of each roll with butter.
    - Toast the rolls in the skillet until golden brown on both sides.
4. **Assemble the Lobster Rolls:**
    - Spoon the lobster mixture into the toasted rolls.
5. **Serve:**
    - Garnish with extra chives or parsley and serve with lemon wedges on the side.

Enjoy your delicious lobster rolls!

## Grilled Tuna Steaks with Soy Ginger Glaze

**Ingredients:**

- **For the Tuna Steaks:**
    - 4 tuna steaks (about 6 oz each), preferably sashimi-grade
    - 2 tbsp olive oil
    - Salt and freshly ground black pepper to taste
- **For the Soy Ginger Glaze:**
    - 1/4 cup soy sauce
    - 2 tbsp honey or brown sugar
    - 2 tbsp rice vinegar
    - 1 tbsp grated fresh ginger
    - 2 cloves garlic, minced
    - 1 tsp sesame oil
    - 1 tsp cornstarch mixed with 1 tbsp water (optional, for thickening)
- **For Garnish:**
    - 1 tbsp sesame seeds
    - 2 green onions, thinly sliced
    - Fresh cilantro or parsley, for garnish (optional)

**Instructions:**

1. **Prepare the Glaze:**
    - In a small saucepan, combine soy sauce, honey (or brown sugar), rice vinegar, grated ginger, minced garlic, and sesame oil.
    - Bring to a simmer over medium heat, stirring frequently.
    - If you prefer a thicker glaze, mix cornstarch with water to form a slurry and add to the saucepan. Simmer for an additional 2-3 minutes until the glaze has thickened slightly.
    - Remove from heat and let cool.
2. **Prepare the Tuna Steaks:**
    - Brush the tuna steaks with olive oil and season with salt and pepper.
3. **Grill the Tuna:**
    - Preheat your grill to high heat.
    - Place the tuna steaks on the grill and cook for 2-3 minutes per side for medium-rare, or longer if you prefer them more cooked. The grill should create a nice sear on the outside while keeping the center rare to medium-rare.
    - Remove from the grill and let rest for a few minutes.
4. **Serve:**
    - Brush the grilled tuna steaks with the soy ginger glaze.
    - Garnish with sesame seeds, sliced green onions, and fresh cilantro or parsley if desired.
    - Serve with extra glaze on the side or over steamed rice or vegetables.

Enjoy your flavorful and succulent grilled tuna steaks with soy ginger glaze!

# Creamy Crab Pasta

## Ingredients:

- 8 oz (225g) pasta (such as fettuccine, linguine, or tagliatelle)
- 1 tbsp olive oil
- 2 cloves garlic, minced
- 1 small shallot, finely chopped
- 1/2 cup white wine (optional)
- 1 cup heavy cream
- 1/2 cup chicken or seafood broth
- 8 oz (225g) crabmeat, picked over for shells
- 1/4 cup grated Parmesan cheese
- 1 tbsp lemon juice
- 1 tbsp chopped fresh parsley
- Salt and freshly ground black pepper to taste

## Instructions:

1. **Cook the Pasta:**
   - In a large pot of salted boiling water, cook the pasta according to package instructions until al dente. Reserve 1/2 cup of pasta cooking water, then drain and set aside.
2. **Prepare the Sauce:**
   - In a large skillet, heat olive oil over medium heat.
   - Add the minced garlic and chopped shallot, cooking until softened and fragrant, about 2-3 minutes.
   - Pour in the white wine (if using) and cook until reduced by half, about 2 minutes.
3. **Make the Cream Sauce:**
   - Add heavy cream and broth to the skillet. Bring to a simmer and cook for 3-4 minutes, until slightly thickened.
   - Stir in the crabmeat and cook gently until heated through, about 2 minutes.
   - Add grated Parmesan cheese, lemon juice, and chopped parsley. Stir to combine. Adjust seasoning with salt and pepper.
4. **Combine Pasta and Sauce:**
   - Toss the cooked pasta in the sauce, adding reserved pasta water a little at a time to reach desired consistency.
5. **Serve:**
   - Serve the creamy crab pasta garnished with extra parsley and Parmesan cheese if desired.

Enjoy your rich and delicious creamy crab pasta!

## Ceviche with Lime and Cilantro

### Ingredients:

- 1 lb (450g) firm white fish (like tilapia, cod, or snapper), cut into small, bite-sized cubes
- 1/2 cup fresh lime juice (about 4-5 limes)
- 1/4 cup fresh lemon juice (about 2 lemons)
- 1 small red onion, finely chopped
- 1-2 serrano or jalapeño peppers, seeded and minced (adjust to heat preference)
- 1 cup cherry tomatoes, diced
- 1/2 cucumber, peeled and diced
- 1/4 cup chopped fresh cilantro
- 1 avocado, diced (optional)
- Salt and freshly ground black pepper to taste

### Instructions:

1. **Marinate the Fish:**
    - In a glass or non-reactive bowl, combine the fish cubes with lime and lemon juice. Make sure the fish is completely submerged in the juice.
    - Cover and refrigerate for 2-3 hours, or until the fish is opaque and firm.
2. **Prepare the Vegetables:**
    - In a separate bowl, mix the chopped red onion, minced peppers, diced cherry tomatoes, cucumber, and cilantro.
3. **Combine and Serve:**
    - Drain the fish from the marinade and gently mix with the vegetable mixture.
    - Add diced avocado if using, and season with salt and pepper to taste.
    - Serve immediately with tortilla chips or as a topping for tostadas.

Enjoy your vibrant and flavorful ceviche with lime and cilantro!

**Baked Salmon with Dill and Lemon**

**Ingredients:**

- 4 salmon fillets (6 oz each), skinless
- 2 tbsp olive oil
- 2 tbsp fresh dill, chopped (or 2 tsp dried dill)
- 1 lemon, thinly sliced
- 2 cloves garlic, minced
- 1/2 tsp paprika (optional)
- Salt and freshly ground black pepper to taste

**Instructions:**

1. **Preheat Oven:**
   - Preheat your oven to 375°F (190°C).
2. **Prepare the Salmon:**
   - Place the salmon fillets on a baking sheet lined with parchment paper or aluminum foil.
   - Brush each fillet with olive oil and season with salt and pepper.
   - Sprinkle minced garlic and paprika (if using) evenly over the fillets.
3. **Add Dill and Lemon:**
   - Sprinkle the chopped dill over the salmon fillets.
   - Lay lemon slices on top of each fillet.
4. **Bake:**
   - Bake in the preheated oven for 15-20 minutes, or until the salmon is cooked through and flakes easily with a fork. The exact cooking time may vary depending on the thickness of the fillets.
5. **Serve:**
   - Serve the salmon with the lemon slices and a sprinkle of extra fresh dill if desired.
   - This dish pairs well with steamed vegetables, rice, or a fresh salad.

Enjoy your delicious and fragrant baked salmon with dill and lemon!

**Bouillabaisse (Provençal Fish Stew)**

**Ingredients:**

- **For the Broth:**
    - 2 tbsp olive oil
    - 1 onion, finely chopped
    - 2 leeks, white and light green parts only, sliced
    - 3 cloves garlic, minced
    - 1 fennel bulb, thinly sliced
    - 1-2 tomatoes, peeled and diced (or 1 can crushed tomatoes)
    - 1/2 cup dry white wine
    - 4 cups fish stock or chicken broth
    - 1/2 tsp saffron threads
    - 1 tsp dried thyme
    - 1 bay leaf
    - Salt and freshly ground black pepper to taste
- **For the Fish and Seafood:**
    - 1 lb (450g) firm white fish (such as cod, snapper, or monkfish), cut into chunks
    - 1/2 lb (225g) mussels, cleaned and debearded
    - 1/2 lb (225g) clams, cleaned
    - 1/2 lb (225g) shrimp, peeled and deveined
- **For Serving:**
    - 1 baguette, sliced and toasted
    - Rouille sauce (optional, for serving)

**Instructions:**

1. **Prepare the Broth:**
    - Heat olive oil in a large pot over medium heat.
    - Add the onion, leeks, and fennel. Cook until softened, about 5-7 minutes.
    - Stir in the garlic and cook for another minute.
    - Add the tomatoes, white wine, and cook for 2-3 minutes until the wine is slightly reduced.
    - Pour in the fish stock or chicken broth, saffron, thyme, and bay leaf. Bring to a boil, then reduce heat and simmer for 20 minutes.
2. **Cook the Seafood:**
    - Add the firm white fish to the pot and simmer for 5 minutes.
    - Add the mussels and clams, cover, and cook for 5-7 minutes, or until they open. Discard any that do not open.
    - Add the shrimp and cook for an additional 3-4 minutes, until pink and cooked through.
3. **Season and Serve:**
    - Remove the bay leaf and adjust seasoning with salt and pepper.

- Serve the bouillabaisse hot, with toasted baguette slices and rouille sauce if desired.

Enjoy your hearty and flavorful bouillabaisse!

**Fried Calamari with Marinara Sauce**

**Ingredients:**

- **For the Calamari:**
    - 1 lb (450g) calamari rings (fresh or thawed)
    - 1 cup all-purpose flour
    - 1 cup cornmeal
    - 1 tsp garlic powder
    - 1 tsp onion powder
    - 1/2 tsp paprika
    - 1/2 tsp dried oregano
    - Salt and freshly ground black pepper to taste
    - Vegetable oil, for frying (such as canola or peanut oil)
- **For the Marinara Sauce:**
    - 1 cup marinara sauce (store-bought or homemade)
    - 1/2 tsp dried basil (optional)
    - 1/2 tsp dried oregano (optional)

**Instructions:**

1. **Prepare the Marinara Sauce:**
    - In a small saucepan, heat marinara sauce over low heat.
    - Stir in dried basil and oregano if desired. Keep warm.
2. **Prepare the Calamari:**
    - In a large bowl, combine flour, cornmeal, garlic powder, onion powder, paprika, oregano, salt, and pepper.
    - Pat the calamari rings dry with paper towels.
    - Dredge the calamari rings in the flour mixture, ensuring they are evenly coated. Shake off excess flour.
3. **Fry the Calamari:**
    - Heat 2-3 inches of vegetable oil in a deep skillet or pot over medium-high heat to 350°F (175°C).
    - Fry the calamari in batches, being careful not to overcrowd the pan. Cook for 1-2 minutes per batch, or until golden brown and crispy.
    - Remove the fried calamari with a slotted spoon and drain on paper towels. Season with a little salt immediately after frying.
4. **Serve:**
    - Arrange the fried calamari on a serving platter.
    - Serve with warm marinara sauce for dipping.

Enjoy your crispy and delicious fried calamari with marinara sauce!

**Garlic Butter Shrimp**

**Ingredients:**

- 1 lb (450g) large shrimp, peeled and deveined
- 3 tbsp unsalted butter
- 4 cloves garlic, minced
- 1/4 cup dry white wine or chicken broth (optional)
- 1/2 tsp red pepper flakes (optional, for heat)
- 1 tbsp fresh lemon juice
- 2 tbsp chopped fresh parsley
- Salt and freshly ground black pepper to taste

**Instructions:**

1. **Cook the Shrimp:**
    - In a large skillet, melt the butter over medium heat.
    - Add the minced garlic and cook for 1-2 minutes until fragrant, being careful not to burn it.
2. **Add the Shrimp:**
    - Add the shrimp to the skillet in a single layer. Cook for 2-3 minutes on each side until pink and opaque.
3. **Deglaze and Finish:**
    - If using, pour in the white wine or chicken broth, and cook for another 1-2 minutes, allowing the sauce to reduce slightly.
    - Stir in the red pepper flakes, lemon juice, and chopped parsley.
    - Season with salt and pepper to taste.
4. **Serve:**
    - Serve the garlic butter shrimp with crusty bread for dipping, over pasta, or alongside vegetables.

Enjoy your rich and flavorful garlic butter shrimp!

# Poke Bowl with Ahi Tuna

**Ingredients:**

- **For the Ahi Tuna:**
    - 1 lb (450g) ahi tuna, sushi-grade, diced
    - 1/4 cup soy sauce
    - 1 tbsp sesame oil
    - 1 tbsp rice vinegar
    - 1 tsp honey or sugar
    - 1 tsp grated ginger
    - 1 tsp sesame seeds
    - 1/2 avocado, diced (optional)
- **For the Bowl:**
    - 2 cups cooked sushi rice or brown rice
    - 1 cup edamame, cooked
    - 1 cup sliced cucumber
    - 1/2 cup shredded carrots
    - 1/2 cup radishes, thinly sliced
    - 1/4 cup seaweed salad
    - 2-3 green onions, sliced
    - Pickled ginger, for garnish (optional)
- **For Garnish (optional):**
    - Additional sesame seeds
    - Sriracha or spicy mayo
    - Fresh cilantro or parsley

**Instructions:**

1. **Marinate the Tuna:**
    - In a bowl, combine soy sauce, sesame oil, rice vinegar, honey, grated ginger, and sesame seeds.
    - Add the diced tuna and gently toss to coat. Let it marinate in the refrigerator for about 15-20 minutes.
2. **Assemble the Bowl:**
    - Divide the cooked rice between bowls.
    - Arrange the marinated tuna and other toppings (edamame, cucumber, carrots, radishes, and seaweed salad) over the rice.
3. **Garnish and Serve:**
    - Top with additional sesame seeds, green onions, and pickled ginger if using.
    - Drizzle with sriracha or spicy mayo if desired.
    - Garnish with fresh cilantro or parsley.

Enjoy your vibrant and customizable poke bowl with ahi tuna!

**Fish Tacos with Cilantro Lime Slaw**

**Ingredients:**

- **For the Fish:**
    - 1 lb (450g) white fish fillets (such as cod, tilapia, or snapper)
    - 1/2 cup all-purpose flour
    - 1/2 cup cornmeal
    - 1 tsp paprika
    - 1/2 tsp garlic powder
    - 1/2 tsp cumin
    - 1/2 tsp salt
    - 1/4 tsp black pepper
    - 1 egg, beaten
    - Vegetable oil, for frying
- **For the Cilantro Lime Slaw:**
    - 4 cups shredded cabbage (green or a mix of green and red)
    - 1/2 cup grated carrots
    - 1/4 cup chopped fresh cilantro
    - 1/4 cup mayonnaise
    - 2 tbsp lime juice
    - 1 tbsp honey
    - Salt and freshly ground black pepper to taste
- **For Serving:**
    - 8 small corn or flour tortillas
    - Lime wedges
    - Extra cilantro for garnish

**Instructions:**

1. **Prepare the Cilantro Lime Slaw:**
    - In a large bowl, combine shredded cabbage, grated carrots, and chopped cilantro.
    - In a small bowl, whisk together mayonnaise, lime juice, honey, salt, and pepper.
    - Toss the slaw with the dressing until well coated. Set aside.
2. **Prepare the Fish:**
    - In a shallow dish, mix flour, cornmeal, paprika, garlic powder, cumin, salt, and pepper.
    - Dip the fish fillets in the beaten egg, then dredge in the flour mixture, coating evenly.
    - Heat vegetable oil in a skillet over medium-high heat.
    - Fry the fish fillets for 3-4 minutes per side, or until golden brown and cooked through. Remove from the skillet and drain on paper towels.
3. **Assemble the Tacos:**

        - Warm the tortillas in a dry skillet or oven.
        - Break the fish into smaller pieces and place on the tortillas.
        - Top with cilantro lime slaw.
4. **Serve:**
        - Garnish with extra cilantro and serve with lime wedges on the side.

Enjoy your flavorful and fresh fish tacos with cilantro lime slaw!

# Lobster Macaroni and Cheese

## Ingredients:

- **For the Mac and Cheese:**
    - 8 oz (225g) elbow macaroni or cavatappi
    - 2 tbsp butter
    - 2 tbsp all-purpose flour
    - 2 cups whole milk
    - 1 cup heavy cream
    - 2 cups sharp cheddar cheese, shredded
    - 1 cup Gruyère cheese, shredded
    - 1/2 cup Parmesan cheese, grated
    - 1/2 tsp garlic powder
    - 1/2 tsp onion powder
    - 1/4 tsp smoked paprika
    - Salt and freshly ground black pepper to taste
    - 1 cup cooked lobster meat, chopped (about 1-2 lobster tails)
- **For the Topping:**
    - 1/2 cup panko breadcrumbs
    - 2 tbsp butter, melted
    - 1/4 cup Parmesan cheese, grated
    - 1 tbsp chopped fresh parsley (optional)

## Instructions:

1. **Cook the Pasta:**
    - Cook the macaroni according to package instructions until al dente. Drain and set aside.
2. **Prepare the Cheese Sauce:**
    - In a large saucepan, melt 2 tbsp butter over medium heat.
    - Stir in the flour and cook for 1-2 minutes to form a roux.
    - Gradually whisk in the milk and cream, and continue to cook, stirring constantly, until the sauce thickens and is smooth.
    - Reduce heat to low and stir in the cheddar, Gruyère, and Parmesan cheeses until melted and smooth.
    - Season with garlic powder, onion powder, smoked paprika, salt, and pepper.
3. **Combine Pasta and Lobster:**
    - Gently fold the cooked macaroni and lobster meat into the cheese sauce until evenly combined.
4. **Prepare the Topping:**
    - In a small bowl, mix the panko breadcrumbs with melted butter and Parmesan cheese.
5. **Bake:**

    - Preheat your oven to 375°F (190°C).
    - Transfer the macaroni and cheese mixture to a baking dish.
    - Sprinkle the breadcrumb mixture evenly over the top.
    - Bake for 20-25 minutes, or until the top is golden brown and the sauce is bubbly.
6. **Serve:**
    - Garnish with chopped parsley if desired and serve hot.

Enjoy your creamy and indulgent lobster macaroni and cheese!

# Poached Salmon with Dill Sauce

## Ingredients:

- **For the Poached Salmon:**
    - 4 salmon fillets (6 oz each), skinless
    - 4 cups water
    - 1 cup dry white wine (or extra water)
    - 1 lemon, sliced
    - 1 small onion, sliced
    - 2 cloves garlic, smashed
    - 2 sprigs fresh dill
    - 1 bay leaf
    - Salt and pepper to taste
- **For the Dill Sauce:**
    - 1 cup sour cream or Greek yogurt
    - 2 tbsp fresh dill, chopped
    - 1 tbsp lemon juice
    - 1 tsp Dijon mustard
    - Salt and pepper to taste

## Instructions:

1. **Poach the Salmon:**
    - In a large skillet or saucepan, combine water, white wine, lemon slices, onion, garlic, dill sprigs, and bay leaf. Bring to a simmer.
    - Season the salmon fillets with salt and pepper. Gently place the fillets in the simmering liquid.
    - Cover and simmer for 8-10 minutes, or until the salmon is cooked through and flakes easily with a fork. Remove the fillets with a slotted spoon and set aside.
2. **Prepare the Dill Sauce:**
    - In a bowl, mix together sour cream, fresh dill, lemon juice, Dijon mustard, salt, and pepper until well combined.
3. **Serve:**
    - Place the poached salmon on plates and serve with a dollop of dill sauce on top or on the side.

Enjoy your light and flavorful poached salmon with dill sauce!

**Crab and Corn Chowder**

**Ingredients:**

- **For the Chowder:**
    - 2 tbsp butter
    - 1 onion, finely chopped
    - 2 cloves garlic, minced
    - 2 celery stalks, diced
    - 1 red bell pepper, diced
    - 2 cups fresh or frozen corn kernels
    - 2 cups diced potatoes
    - 3 cups seafood or chicken broth
    - 1 cup heavy cream
    - 1 cup cooked crab meat, picked over for shells
    - 1 tsp Old Bay seasoning (optional)
    - 1/2 tsp paprika
    - 1/4 tsp cayenne pepper (optional, for heat)
    - Salt and freshly ground black pepper to taste
    - 2 tbsp chopped fresh parsley (for garnish)

**Instructions:**

1. **Sauté the Vegetables:**
    - In a large pot, melt butter over medium heat.
    - Add onion, garlic, celery, and red bell pepper. Cook until softened, about 5 minutes.
2. **Add Corn and Potatoes:**
    - Stir in corn and potatoes, cooking for another 2 minutes.
3. **Simmer the Chowder:**
    - Add the broth and bring to a boil.
    - Reduce heat and simmer until potatoes are tender, about 15-20 minutes.
4. **Finish the Chowder:**
    - Stir in heavy cream and crab meat. Add Old Bay seasoning, paprika, and cayenne pepper if using.
    - Simmer for 5 minutes to heat through and meld flavors. Adjust seasoning with salt and pepper.
5. **Serve:**
    - Ladle the chowder into bowls and garnish with chopped parsley.

Enjoy your creamy and flavorful crab and corn chowder!

**Oysters on the Half Shell**

**Ingredients:**

- Fresh oysters, shucked (as many as you need)
- Lemon wedges, for garnish
- Freshly grated horseradish (optional)
- Hot sauce (such as Tabasco), for serving
- Mignonette sauce (optional, recipe below)

**Mignonette Sauce:**

- 1/4 cup red wine vinegar
- 2 tbsp finely minced shallots
- 1 tbsp freshly ground black pepper
- 1 tsp sugar (optional)

**Instructions:**

1. **Shuck the Oysters:**
   - Place the oysters in a bowl of ice to chill. This makes them easier to handle.
   - Use an oyster knife to shuck the oysters. Insert the knife into the hinge of the oyster and twist to open. Be careful to keep the oyster liquor (the liquid inside) in the shell.
   - Remove the top shell and carefully detach the oyster from the bottom shell, keeping it in place.
2. **Prepare the Mignonette Sauce (if using):**
   - In a small bowl, mix red wine vinegar, minced shallots, black pepper, and sugar if using. Let it sit for at least 15 minutes to allow the flavors to meld.
3. **Serve the Oysters:**
   - Arrange the shucked oysters on a platter lined with crushed ice or rock salt to keep them steady.
   - Garnish with lemon wedges.
   - Serve with optional mignonette sauce, freshly grated horseradish, and hot sauce.
4. **Enjoy:**
   - To eat, simply take the oyster with a small fork or by lifting it with the shell, and enjoy the fresh, briny flavor.

Oysters on the half shell are best enjoyed fresh and chilled. They pair wonderfully with crisp white wines or champagne.

## Grilled Sardines with Lemon and Herbs

### Ingredients:

- 1 lb (450g) fresh sardines, cleaned and gutted
- 2 tbsp olive oil
- 2 cloves garlic, minced
- 1 lemon, thinly sliced
- 2 tbsp fresh parsley, chopped
- 1 tbsp fresh thyme leaves (or 1 tsp dried thyme)
- Salt and freshly ground black pepper to taste
- Lemon wedges, for serving

### Instructions:

1. **Prepare the Sardines:**
    - Rinse the sardines under cold water and pat dry with paper towels.
2. **Marinate:**
    - In a small bowl, mix olive oil, minced garlic, chopped parsley, and thyme. Season with salt and pepper.
    - Rub the sardines with the olive oil mixture, making sure to coat both inside and out. Let them marinate for about 15-30 minutes.
3. **Grill:**
    - Preheat your grill to medium-high heat.
    - Place the sardines on the grill. Grill for 2-3 minutes per side, or until the skin is crispy and the fish is cooked through.
4. **Serve:**
    - Transfer the grilled sardines to a serving platter.
    - Garnish with lemon slices and additional chopped parsley if desired.
    - Serve with lemon wedges on the side.

Enjoy your delicious and aromatic grilled sardines with lemon and herbs!

# Clams Casino

## Ingredients:

- 12 large clams (littleneck or cherrystone), scrubbed clean
- 4 slices bacon, diced
- 1/2 cup breadcrumbs (preferably Italian or panko)
- 1/4 cup grated Parmesan cheese
- 2 cloves garlic, minced
- 1/4 cup chopped fresh parsley
- 1/4 cup finely diced red bell pepper
- 1 tbsp lemon juice
- 2 tbsp butter, melted
- Salt and freshly ground black pepper to taste
- Lemon wedges, for serving

## Instructions:

1. **Prepare the Clams:**
   - Preheat your oven to 375°F (190°C).
   - In a large pot, steam the clams over medium heat for about 5-7 minutes, or until they open. Discard any clams that do not open.
   - Remove the clams from their shells, being careful to retain the clam meat and discard the top shell. Place the clam meat back into the bottom shell.
2. **Make the Topping:**
   - In a skillet over medium heat, cook the diced bacon until crispy. Remove the bacon with a slotted spoon and drain on paper towels. Discard excess fat from the skillet.
   - Add minced garlic to the same skillet and cook for about 1 minute, until fragrant.
   - In a bowl, combine breadcrumbs, grated Parmesan cheese, cooked bacon, garlic, chopped parsley, diced red bell pepper, lemon juice, and melted butter. Mix until well combined. Season with salt and pepper to taste.
3. **Assemble and Bake:**
   - Spoon the breadcrumb mixture evenly over each clam.
   - Place the clams on a baking sheet and bake in the preheated oven for 10-12 minutes, or until the topping is golden and crispy.
4. **Serve:**
   - Serve the clams casino hot, garnished with lemon wedges on the side.

Enjoy your flavorful and crispy clams casino!

## Curry Crab Legs

### Ingredients:

- 2 lbs (900g) crab legs (king or snow crab)
- 2 tbsp vegetable oil
- 1 onion, finely chopped
- 3 cloves garlic, minced
- 1 tbsp fresh ginger, minced
- 2 tbsp curry powder (adjust to taste)
- 1/2 tsp ground turmeric
- 1/2 tsp ground cumin
- 1/2 tsp paprika
- 1 cup coconut milk
- 1/2 cup chicken or seafood broth
- 1 tbsp soy sauce
- 1 tbsp lime juice
- 1 tbsp brown sugar
- 1-2 tsp red chili flakes or hot sauce (optional, for heat)
- Salt and freshly ground black pepper to taste
- Fresh cilantro or parsley, for garnish
- Lime wedges, for serving

### Instructions:

1. **Prepare the Crab Legs:**
   - If the crab legs are frozen, thaw them in the refrigerator overnight or under cold running water.
   - Crack the crab legs slightly to allow the curry sauce to penetrate.
2. **Make the Curry Sauce:**
   - In a large skillet or pot, heat vegetable oil over medium heat.
   - Add the chopped onion and cook until softened, about 5 minutes.
   - Stir in the minced garlic and ginger, and cook for another minute.
   - Add curry powder, turmeric, cumin, and paprika. Cook for 1-2 minutes, until fragrant.
3. **Add Liquids:**
   - Pour in the coconut milk and chicken or seafood broth. Stir well to combine.
   - Add soy sauce, lime juice, brown sugar, and red chili flakes or hot sauce if using. Bring to a simmer.
   - Adjust seasoning with salt and pepper.
4. **Cook the Crab Legs:**
   - Add the crab legs to the skillet or pot, making sure they are coated with the sauce.

- Cover and simmer for 10-15 minutes, or until the crab legs are heated through and the sauce has thickened slightly.

5. **Serve:**
    - Transfer the crab legs to a serving platter.
    - Spoon the curry sauce over the crab legs.
    - Garnish with chopped fresh cilantro or parsley and serve with lime wedges.

Enjoy your flavorful and aromatic curry crab legs!

## Sautéed Mussels with Garlic and Herbs

### Ingredients:

- 2 lbs (900g) fresh mussels, scrubbed and debearded
- 2 tbsp olive oil
- 4 cloves garlic, minced
- 1 shallot, finely chopped (optional)
- 1/2 cup white wine (or chicken broth)
- 1/2 cup chicken or seafood broth
- 1/4 cup fresh parsley, chopped
- 1 tbsp fresh thyme leaves (or 1 tsp dried thyme)
- 1/2 tsp red pepper flakes (optional, for heat)
- Salt and freshly ground black pepper to taste
- Lemon wedges, for serving
- Crusty bread, for serving (optional)

### Instructions:

1. **Prepare the Mussels:**
   - Rinse the mussels under cold water. Scrub the shells with a brush and remove any beards. Discard any mussels that are open and do not close when tapped.
2. **Sauté the Aromatics:**
   - In a large skillet or pot, heat olive oil over medium heat.
   - Add the minced garlic and chopped shallot (if using) and cook for 1-2 minutes, until fragrant but not browned.
3. **Cook the Mussels:**
   - Add the white wine and broth to the skillet. Bring to a simmer.
   - Add the mussels to the skillet, cover, and cook for 5-7 minutes, or until the mussels have opened. Discard any mussels that do not open.
4. **Finish the Dish:**
   - Stir in the chopped parsley, thyme, and red pepper flakes (if using). Season with salt and pepper to taste.
   - Let the mussels cook for an additional 1-2 minutes to meld the flavors.
5. **Serve:**
   - Transfer the mussels and broth to a serving bowl or platter.
   - Serve with lemon wedges and crusty bread for dipping into the flavorful broth.

Enjoy your delicious and aromatic sautéed mussels with garlic and herbs!

**Crab-Stuffed Avocados**

**Ingredients:**

- 2 ripe avocados, halved and pitted
- 1 cup cooked crab meat, picked over for shells
- 1/4 cup mayonnaise
- 1 tbsp fresh lemon juice
- 1 tbsp Dijon mustard
- 1 celery stalk, finely diced
- 1/4 cup red bell pepper, finely diced
- 2 tbsp fresh chives or parsley, chopped
- 1/2 tsp Old Bay seasoning (optional)
- Salt and freshly ground black pepper to taste

**Instructions:**

1. **Prepare the Crab Filling:**
    - In a bowl, combine crab meat, mayonnaise, lemon juice, Dijon mustard, diced celery, diced red bell pepper, and chopped chives or parsley.
    - Season with Old Bay seasoning (if using), salt, and pepper. Mix gently until well combined.
2. **Stuff the Avocados:**
    - Scoop a small amount of the crab mixture into each avocado half, mounding it slightly.
3. **Serve:**
    - Arrange the stuffed avocados on a serving platter.
    - Garnish with additional chives or parsley if desired.

Enjoy your light and flavorful crab-stuffed avocados!

**Tuna Poke Nachos**

**Ingredients:**

- **For the Tuna Poke:**
    - 1 lb (450g) sushi-grade tuna, diced
    - 1/4 cup soy sauce
    - 1 tbsp sesame oil
    - 1 tbsp rice vinegar
    - 1 tsp honey or sugar
    - 1 tsp freshly grated ginger
    - 1/2 avocado, diced
    - 1 small cucumber, thinly sliced
    - 1/4 cup scallions, thinly sliced
    - 1 tsp sesame seeds
    - 1 tsp red pepper flakes (optional, for heat)
- **For the Nachos:**
    - 1 bag tortilla chips (about 12 oz)
    - 1 cup shredded cheese (cheddar, Monterey Jack, or a blend)
    - 1/2 cup pickled jalapeños (optional)
    - 1/4 cup sliced black olives (optional)
- **For Garnish:**
    - 1/4 cup chopped fresh cilantro
    - Lime wedges
    - Additional soy sauce or ponzu sauce, for drizzling

**Instructions:**

1. **Prepare the Tuna Poke:**
    - In a bowl, combine soy sauce, sesame oil, rice vinegar, honey, and grated ginger. Mix well.
    - Add the diced tuna to the bowl and gently toss to coat.
    - Stir in diced avocado, sliced cucumber, scallions, sesame seeds, and red pepper flakes (if using). Set aside.
2. **Prepare the Nachos:**
    - Preheat your oven to 375°F (190°C).
    - Spread the tortilla chips in a single layer on a baking sheet.
    - Sprinkle the shredded cheese evenly over the chips.
    - Bake for 5-7 minutes, or until the cheese is melted and bubbly.
3. **Assemble the Nachos:**
    - Remove the nachos from the oven and let them cool slightly.
    - Spoon the tuna poke mixture evenly over the nachos.
    - Add pickled jalapeños and sliced black olives if desired.
4. **Garnish and Serve:**

- Garnish with chopped cilantro.
- Drizzle with additional soy sauce or ponzu sauce if desired.
- Serve with lime wedges on the side for a fresh squeeze of citrus.

Enjoy your creative and delicious tuna poke nachos!

## Spicy Shrimp Tostadas

**Ingredients:**

- **For the Shrimp:**
    - 1 lb (450g) large shrimp, peeled and deveined
    - 2 tbsp olive oil
    - 1 tbsp chili powder
    - 1 tsp paprika
    - 1/2 tsp cayenne pepper (adjust to taste)
    - 1/2 tsp garlic powder
    - 1/2 tsp onion powder
    - Salt and freshly ground black pepper to taste
- **For the Tostadas:**
    - 4-6 tostada shells (store-bought or homemade)
    - 1 cup shredded lettuce
    - 1 cup diced tomatoes
    - 1/2 cup thinly sliced red onion
    - 1 avocado, sliced
    - 1/4 cup chopped fresh cilantro
    - Lime wedges, for serving
- **For the Sauce (optional):**
    - 1/2 cup sour cream or Greek yogurt
    - 1 tbsp lime juice
    - 1 tbsp chopped fresh cilantro
    - 1/2 tsp hot sauce (optional)

**Instructions:**

1. **Prepare the Shrimp:**
    - In a bowl, toss the shrimp with olive oil, chili powder, paprika, cayenne pepper, garlic powder, onion powder, salt, and pepper.
    - Heat a skillet over medium-high heat and cook the shrimp for 2-3 minutes per side, or until pink and cooked through. Remove from heat.
2. **Prepare the Sauce (if using):**
    - In a small bowl, mix sour cream or Greek yogurt with lime juice, chopped cilantro, and hot sauce if desired. Adjust seasoning as needed.
3. **Assemble the Tostadas:**
    - Place the tostada shells on a serving platter.
    - Spread a layer of shredded lettuce on each tostada.
    - Top with diced tomatoes, sliced red onion, and avocado slices.
    - Arrange the cooked shrimp on top of the vegetables.
4. **Garnish and Serve:**
    - Drizzle with the prepared sauce if using, or serve it on the side.

- Garnish with chopped cilantro and serve with lime wedges.

Enjoy your crispy and spicy shrimp tostadas!

**Fish en Papillote (Fish in Paper)**

**Ingredients:**

- 4 fish fillets (such as cod, salmon, or tilapia)
- 1 lemon, thinly sliced
- 1 zucchini, thinly sliced
- 1 red bell pepper, thinly sliced
- 1 small carrot, julienned
- 2 cloves garlic, minced
- 2 tbsp olive oil
- 2 tbsp fresh parsley, chopped
- 1 tbsp fresh thyme leaves (or 1 tsp dried thyme)
- Salt and freshly ground black pepper to taste
- 4 large sheets of parchment paper (or aluminum foil if parchment isn't available)

**Instructions:**

1. **Preheat the Oven:**
   - Preheat your oven to 400°F (200°C).
2. **Prepare the Parchment Paper:**
   - Cut four large sheets of parchment paper, about 12-14 inches long. Fold each sheet in half and then unfold to create a crease. This will help with folding the packets later.
3. **Assemble the Packets:**
   - On one half of each parchment sheet, place a portion of the zucchini, red bell pepper, and carrot.
   - Drizzle with a little olive oil and season with salt and pepper.
   - Place a fish fillet on top of the vegetables.
   - Season the fish with minced garlic, fresh parsley, thyme, salt, and pepper.
   - Top the fish with lemon slices.
   - Drizzle with a little more olive oil.
4. **Seal the Packets:**
   - Fold the other half of the parchment paper over the fish and vegetables, creating a closed packet. Starting at one end, fold the edges of the parchment paper to seal the packet tightly. You should end up with a semi-circular or oval-shaped packet.
   - Repeat with the remaining ingredients.
5. **Bake:**
   - Place the packets on a baking sheet and bake in the preheated oven for 15-20 minutes, or until the fish is cooked through and flakes easily with a fork. The vegetables should also be tender.
6. **Serve:**

- Carefully open the packets (be cautious of steam) and transfer the contents to plates.
- Serve directly from the parchment or transfer to serving dishes.

## Tips:

- You can customize the vegetables and herbs based on what you have available or your preferences.
- For extra flavor, add a splash of white wine or a squeeze of lemon juice before sealing the packets.

Enjoy your delicious and aromatic fish en papillote!

## Lobster Ravioli with Sage Butter

**Ingredients:**

- **For the Ravioli:**
    - 1 lb (450g) lobster ravioli (store-bought or homemade)
- **For the Sage Butter:**
    - 1/2 cup unsalted butter
    - 10-12 fresh sage leaves
    - 2 cloves garlic, minced
    - 1/4 cup grated Parmesan cheese (optional)
    - Salt and freshly ground black pepper to taste
- **For Garnish:**
    - Fresh sage leaves, fried or crispy (optional)
    - Extra grated Parmesan cheese (optional)

**Instructions:**

1. **Cook the Ravioli:**
    - Bring a large pot of salted water to a boil.
    - Add the lobster ravioli and cook according to the package instructions, usually about 3-4 minutes. Gently stir to prevent sticking.
    - Drain the ravioli and set aside.
2. **Prepare the Sage Butter:**
    - In a large skillet, melt the butter over medium heat.
    - Add the fresh sage leaves and cook for 1-2 minutes, or until they become crispy. Remove the sage leaves from the skillet and set aside.
    - Add the minced garlic to the skillet and cook for 1 minute, or until fragrant.
    - Stir in the cooked ravioli and toss gently to coat with the sage butter.
    - Season with salt and pepper to taste. If using, add the grated Parmesan cheese and toss until melted and combined.
3. **Serve:**
    - Divide the ravioli among serving plates.
    - Drizzle with additional sage butter from the skillet.
    - Garnish with crispy sage leaves and extra Parmesan cheese if desired.

Enjoy your elegant and flavorful lobster ravioli with sage butter!

# Szechuan Peppercorn Shrimp

**Ingredients:**

- **For the Shrimp:**
    - 1 lb (450g) large shrimp, peeled and deveined
    - 2 tbsp cornstarch
    - 1 tbsp soy sauce
    - 1 tbsp rice wine or dry sherry
    - 1 tbsp vegetable oil
- **For the Sauce:**
    - 2 tbsp vegetable oil
    - 2 tbsp Szechuan peppercorns
    - 3-4 dried red chilies (adjust to taste)
    - 2 cloves garlic, minced
    - 1 inch piece of ginger, minced
    - 1/4 cup soy sauce
    - 2 tbsp rice vinegar
    - 2 tbsp hoisin sauce
    - 1 tbsp chili paste or sauce (optional, for extra heat)
    - 1 tsp sugar
    - 1/2 cup water or chicken broth
    - 1-2 tbsp cornstarch mixed with 2 tbsp water (for thickening)
- **For Garnish:**
    - Chopped green onions
    - Fresh cilantro (optional)
    - Cooked rice, for serving

**Instructions:**

1. **Prepare the Shrimp:**
    - In a bowl, toss the shrimp with cornstarch, soy sauce, and rice wine. Let it marinate for about 15 minutes.
2. **Cook the Shrimp:**
    - Heat vegetable oil in a large skillet or wok over medium-high heat.
    - Add the marinated shrimp and cook for 2-3 minutes per side, or until pink and cooked through. Remove from the skillet and set aside.
3. **Make the Sauce:**
    - In the same skillet, add 2 tbsp vegetable oil.
    - Add Szechuan peppercorns and dried red chilies. Stir-fry for 1-2 minutes until fragrant.
    - Add minced garlic and ginger, and cook for another 30 seconds.
    - Stir in soy sauce, rice vinegar, hoisin sauce, chili paste (if using), sugar, and water or chicken broth. Bring to a simmer.

- Stir in the cornstarch mixture to thicken the sauce. Cook for 1-2 minutes until the sauce is glossy and thickened.
4. **Combine and Serve:**
    - Return the cooked shrimp to the skillet and toss to coat in the sauce.
    - Cook for another minute to ensure the shrimp are heated through.
    - Garnish with chopped green onions and fresh cilantro if desired.
5. **Serve:**
    - Serve the Szechuan peppercorn shrimp over cooked rice.

Enjoy your spicy and flavorful Szechuan peppercorn shrimp!

# Teriyaki Glazed Salmon

**Ingredients:**

- **For the Teriyaki Sauce:**
    - 1/2 cup soy sauce
    - 1/4 cup mirin (Japanese sweet rice wine) or dry white wine
    - 1/4 cup honey or brown sugar
    - 2 tbsp rice vinegar
    - 2 cloves garlic, minced
    - 1 tbsp freshly grated ginger
    - 1 tbsp cornstarch mixed with 2 tbsp water (optional, for thickening)
- **For the Salmon:**
    - 4 salmon fillets (about 6 oz each)
    - 1 tbsp olive oil
    - Salt and freshly ground black pepper to taste
    - Sesame seeds and chopped green onions for garnish (optional)

**Instructions:**

1. **Make the Teriyaki Sauce:**
    - In a saucepan, combine soy sauce, mirin, honey or brown sugar, rice vinegar, minced garlic, and grated ginger.
    - Bring to a simmer over medium heat, stirring occasionally.
    - If you prefer a thicker sauce, stir in the cornstarch mixture and cook for another 1-2 minutes until the sauce has thickened.
    - Remove from heat and set aside.
2. **Prepare the Salmon:**
    - Preheat your oven to 375°F (190°C) or preheat your grill.
    - Pat the salmon fillets dry with paper towels and season with salt and pepper.
3. **Cook the Salmon:**
    - **Oven Method:**
        - Heat olive oil in an oven-safe skillet over medium-high heat. Sear the salmon fillets, skin-side down, for about 3-4 minutes until the skin is crispy.
        - Brush a generous amount of teriyaki sauce over the top of the salmon.
        - Transfer the skillet to the preheated oven and bake for 10-12 minutes, or until the salmon is cooked through and flakes easily with a fork.
    - **Grill Method:**
        - Preheat the grill to medium-high heat.
        - Brush the grill grates with oil to prevent sticking.
        - Place the salmon fillets on the grill, skin-side down. Grill for 4-5 minutes per side, or until the salmon is cooked through and has grill marks.
        - Brush with teriyaki sauce during the last few minutes of grilling.

4. **Serve:**
    - Transfer the salmon fillets to serving plates.
    - Drizzle with additional teriyaki sauce.
    - Garnish with sesame seeds and chopped green onions if desired.
    - Serve with steamed rice and vegetables or a fresh salad.

Enjoy your delicious teriyaki glazed salmon!

**Seafood Gumbo**

**Ingredients:**

- **For the Roux:**
    - 1/2 cup vegetable oil
    - 1/2 cup all-purpose flour
- **For the Gumbo:**
    - 1 large onion, diced
    - 1 bell pepper, diced
    - 3 celery stalks, diced
    - 4 cloves garlic, minced
    - 1 (14.5 oz) can diced tomatoes
    - 4 cups seafood stock (or chicken stock)
    - 2 bay leaves
    - 1 tsp dried thyme
    - 1 tsp paprika
    - 1/2 tsp cayenne pepper (adjust to taste)
    - 1 tsp Creole seasoning (or Cajun seasoning)
    - 1 lb (450g) shrimp, peeled and deveined
    - 1/2 lb (225g) crab meat, picked over for shells
    - 1/2 lb (225g) oysters, shucked
    - 1/2 cup chopped fresh parsley
    - 4 green onions, sliced
    - 2 cups okra, sliced (optional, for traditional gumbo)
    - Salt and freshly ground black pepper to taste
    - Cooked white rice, for serving

**Instructions:**

1. **Make the Roux:**
    - In a large pot or Dutch oven, heat the vegetable oil over medium heat.
    - Gradually whisk in the flour, cooking and stirring constantly.
    - Continue to cook, stirring frequently, until the roux is a deep brown color, about 15-20 minutes. Be careful not to burn it.
2. **Cook the Vegetables:**
    - Add the diced onion, bell pepper, and celery to the roux. Cook for 5-7 minutes, until the vegetables are softened.
    - Stir in the minced garlic and cook for another minute.
3. **Add the Liquid and Seasonings:**
    - Stir in the diced tomatoes, seafood stock, bay leaves, dried thyme, paprika, cayenne pepper, and Creole seasoning.
    - Bring to a simmer and cook for 15-20 minutes to let the flavors meld.
4. **Add the Seafood:**

- Add the shrimp, crab meat, and oysters. If using okra, add it at this stage.
- Simmer for another 5-7 minutes, until the seafood is cooked through and the shrimp are pink.

5. **Finish and Serve:**
    - Stir in the chopped parsley and sliced green onions.
    - Adjust seasoning with salt and pepper to taste.
    - Serve the gumbo over cooked white rice.

## Tips:

- **Roux Consistency:** The roux is the base of the gumbo and gives it its rich flavor and color. It's important to cook it to the right color (a deep brown) for the best results.
- **Seafood Variety:** You can customize the seafood based on availability or personal preference, adding ingredients like crawfish or mussels if desired.

Enjoy your hearty and flavorful seafood gumbo!